A
Spark of
Energy
JUST LIKE YOU

VANDA VALENTE

BALBOA.
PRESS

A DIVISION OF HAY HOUSE

Balboa Press books may be ordered through booksellers or by contacting:

Balboa Press
A Division of Hay House
1663 Liberty Drive
Bloomington, IN 47403
www.balboapress.com
1 (877) 407-4847

Because of the dynamic nature of the Internet, any web addresses or
links contained in this book may have changed since publication and
may no longer be valid. The views expressed in this work are solely those
of the author and do not necessarily reflect the views of the publisher,
and the publisher hereby disclaims any responsibility for them.

The author of this book does not dispense medical advice or prescribe the use
of any technique as a form of treatment for physical, emotional, or medical
problems without the advice of a physician, either directly or indirectly. The
intent of the author is only to offer information of a general nature to help
you in your quest for emotional and spiritual well-being. In the event you use
any of the information in this book for yourself, which is your constitutional
right, the author and the publisher assume no responsibility for your actions.

Print information available on the last page.

ISBN: 978-1-9822-0423-5 (sc)
ISBN: 978-1-9822-0422-8 (e)

Balboa Press rev. date: 06/11/2018

"If you want to find the secrets of the universe, think in terms of energy, frequency and vibration."
– Nikola Tesla

Nikola Tesla was a man of science who was not only an electrical and mechanical engineer, but also a physicist and a man with futuristic ideas and projects.

This book is not my story. Even though it is written in the first person, within it you will find reflections and features of the many stories that have crossed my path and that for one reason or another, helped me find my true vibration in the immense vibrational Universe that surrounds us. Thank you for sharing your stories with me. This book is for all of you.

Contents

About this book

In 2008 I started to revolutionise my life, hoping to improve my health and achieve a more balanced lifestyle. My armour was comprised of two things: a deep desire to dispose of miscellaneous health issues that were turning my life into a nightmare, and a voice within telling me that I could succeed because I was much more than a physical machine.

Like many of you, my journey began with dietary changes, but with time I realised that food and supplements, although important, were not enough to take me to the healthy, peaceful place that was secretly vibrating within me, and that I so eagerly wanted to encounter.

My health was improving, but I felt as if only one part of me was recovering and that the physical detox that I was experiencing was insufficient. My heart wanted to detox, my thoughts wanted to detox, and I felt that I had to find an explanation for what I was feeling.

My awareness of a more complete approach to balanced living started slowly, as I explored books about Energy Therapies, brain function, Psychology and Biology. These guided me to incorporate healthier recipes into my daily routine, as well as to acknowledge the inner significance of established behaviours and thought processes, and how they influenced my health.

The human brain has more than 100 billion neurons; each neuron is connected to 10 thousand other neurons. This means that through electrical impulses, neurotransmissions and frequencies, every cell in our body is informed of how we think and feel about ourselves. I didn't know this in the beginning, but when I learned about it, everything changed.

I came to understand that our bodies constantly emanate different frequencies of information to function, to keep us aware of our emotions and thoughts, but also to connect us to the universe. All in energy!

I knew why healthy eating was of great importance, but this alone was not enough to take me to an optimum level of health. What I thought and how I felt would **directly** influence my physical health and *what I did to cleanse blocked patterns was the key to my treasure.*

However, it was only when I read a book about Quantum Physics and Einstein's Theory of Relativity that all of these different perceptions were united and all the levels of my existence became interconnected, giving me a complete perspective of the bodily, mental, emotional and spiritual manifestations within myself. In order to cleanse blocked patterns I needed to address all of these levels, always in the same base and always within the same frequency.

If you are searching for this special and unique place too, either because you are dealing with health issues or are simply in need of a more positive path, you are holding the right book. With this book you will learn why eating healthily and exercising is not enough to overcome health issues. You will understand that you have four different levels within your existence that work together as a whole to keep you healthy and balanced. However, above all you will learn that you are energy and that it is by accepting the uniqueness of your vibration that you will be able to balance all of these levels and feel whole.

I will take you on a journey to the beginning of who you are energetically, and how by understanding this you will grasp the full meaning of **giving life your 100%**. You will realise that this 100% can only be achieved by bringing to your day-to-day routine a harmonic positive input to healthy eating, exercising, emotional and mental cleansing, and connection to the different levels of consciousness that constitute your spiritual level.

In some ways the journeys of learning I undertook felt long and at times painful. When you are holding in your hands a bouquet of chronic illnesses that leave you in agonising pain, fatigue and short-term memory loss, you want things to happen fast. But on reflection it took the time it needed and I grew stronger every step of the way.

I would like for you to have a shorter journey in finding your balance and in finding yourself. By giving you a base of your whole, with a few simple tips and exercises, I hope that you can fly to your peaceful and happy place quickly and that you can appreciate life and the universe around you.

This book is not long (as I shall explain in the following section) but it is the result of a mind that decided never to let go, and even though it can sometimes be forgetful, it found new directions and new information, creating new neurological pathways that spread its positive energy throughout the body and creating in turn a new life.

The book you are holding is not the answer to everything, but it carries a small spark of information that can take you to the miracle that you are, giving you the chance to find the best approaches to support the whole of your health.

Why such a short book?

When I decided to write this book, my goal was to write something uncomplicated about energy. I knew that it was of extreme importance for people's healthy living to understand that we are vibrational beings, and so it was crucial to write something simple, accessible and not excessively long.

It's true that I refer to Quantum Physics and Biology, but not in the way usually depicted in scientific books. Some of you might even find my approach too simplistic and not as accurate as you would expect. However, my goal is that those of you who feel there is more to your existence than just a physical body understand that the intuition or sixth sense you perceive as guidance represents a form of energy, and that this energy is real and a part of who you are. I want you to know that by grasping the simple idea of atoms and universal energy, and by seeing yourself as a vibrational being living in a vibrational world, this energy will no longer be a 'fantasy' but instead a pure fact and a reality that needs to be taken into consideration on a regular basis.

My approach to meditation is also addressed in a very straightforward way in this book. I believe that meditation is a very important tool for healthy living and I refer to its benefits in detail. However, meditation does not have to be long or require numerous specific rituals. I believe that within ourselves exists a guide of how each person 'should' meditate, and that we simply need to let go of our conscious everyday thoughts. Crucially, this can be done with 'traditional' meditation poses, painting, dancing, walking and even doing the dishes. Just let go and be with yourself!

Please understand, however, that I am not in any way dismissing the importance of meditation as a more profound practice for relaxing, healing and connecting to a higher frequency. In fact, quite the opposite: a lot of my work is based on this profound approach and in my daily routine deep meditation helps me with both my mental and physical balance.

Nonetheless, what I find is that because people are busy and find it difficult to stop and meditate, they do not do it and do not even come close to any type of routine that could activate their inner energy.

Therefore, my goal here is to give you easy exercises that will activate a meditative feeling, because this way you will naturally and slowly bring to your life a deeper sense of calmness and closeness to your energetic uniqueness. Who knows, over time the need for a more profound form of meditation will arise and you will take the next step.

Whatever meditative approach you decide to take, the important thing is to never give up on the search for your own health path, your own vibration, because to go through life unaware of your profound connection to everything that surrounds you means missing out on the full potential of your physical existence and what you can learn with it.

Seeing ourselves as an energetic dance between the

different levels that constitute our being and living (physical, mental, emotional and spiritual), can make our journey easier, healthier, more compassionate and meaningful!

I believe that if people are given the chance to learn in a simple, straightforward way that we are made of energy at a subatomic level and that because of this we are one with the universe around us, this process of change will become easier and the world will be a better place.

This is why I wrote this book. It is a simple approach to the energetic base of our existence, how it connects us to the universe and how it makes us unique, but never alone.

It won't take you long to go through my sea of words, so take your time, read slowly. Absorb the information, and above all feel special. So special that you will want to take better care of your body, letting go of negative thought patterns and emotions and giving yourself the chance to love and feel good, because you are a walking miracle!

Three important notes before you continue:

- When I refer to spiritual or spirituality, I am referring to those dimensions that Quantum Physics explains as realms where time as we conceive it, with future and past, exists all in the now and where form and space are purely mental constructs.

- For our quick analysis, please just see **mass/matter** as anything 'physical', as for example your body, animals, objects.

- Frequency: We are made of energy. Everything around us is energy because atoms are the base of everything in the universe. These atoms are in constant state of motion, entangling in different ways. Depending on the speed of these atoms, things appear as solid, liquid, or gas. They vibrate in different ways, emanating a different frequency. Everything in nature vibrates at different frequencies, including us and each part of our body and even our thoughts. It's like an orchestra playing a melody, but each instrument emanating its own frequency!

"There is a force in the universe, which, if we permit, will flow through us and produce miraculous results."
Mahatma Gandhi

We are energy

I remember the day, nine years ago, when I arrived home after an intense morning in the hospital doing tests. My body was hurting so much that I could hardly walk. My children were asleep, so I ventured to the terrace to feel the warmth of the sun shining outside. I must confess that I'm not sure why I decided to do it – going to bed seemed like a better option – but the cells in my body were desperately asking for the sun and I 'heard' them.

I forced myself to sit in the Sukhasana position, like the Buddha, and just stayed there. The sun was warm and my whole body was absorbing its warmth as if it was food, light and healing, and I remained there. At first it was very uncomfortable, but then ... oh, then it was bliss. My breathing was calm, I started imagining light coming through my head and for one moment, a single, precious, unforgettable moment, I was free of pain. I felt at 'home'!

Years later, this meditative pose continues to bring me to the same place and further.

Looking at the stars also takes me to this place; I feel calm and connected to 'home'. Going to the beach on a summer's day and feeling the warmth of the sun on my skin while walking with my feet in the water makes me feel the same way, calm and connected to 'home'. Closing my eyes while meditating in the garden also connects me to 'home'. Place me among the ones I love ... and I'm 'home'.

Do you ever feel this way? It doesn't matter where or how, but do you ever feel connected to everything, calm, vibrating in a frequency that is so complete that it makes you wonder: Where does this feeling come from? Why do I feel like this?

If you do, I'm sure you're like me and you incorporate in your daily routine a desire to find the answers to these questions, to find yourself and to find a way to be happy, healthy and above all connected; connected to yourself, to the universe, to your uniqueness.

This need might have been intensified by illness or unhappiness, but the truth is that without this 'connection' we feel incomplete, as if a part of us is lost and so we don't feel whole. I always say it is a search for that one moment when our soul, that energetic part of us that seems to know who we are, comes and sits in our heart and everything is fine. We're home!

In my search I have learned that I can look inside myself to find balance, and I have learned that I can also look from within to the outside of myself to find balance, as the reason why we feel this need to be connected is because the universe vibrates within us. Moments like the ones described above are simply *the whole* of you vibrating in a higher frequency of energy, nothing more.

I have learned that no matter what, **the key to my uniqueness and to who I am is in the *Energy*.** By balancing the different frequencies within my existence, I feel at peace and connected to the energy within myself but also to the energy that surrounds me, because the energies that constitute the universe also co-exist within my vibration, so therefore I can also find myself outside of my physical body. How is that possible, you're thinking?

Well, let me share with you a small equation that has changed my life and that derives from the special theory of relativity presented by Einstein: $E=mc^2$.

When you read Einstein's notes on this equation the equivalence of mass and energy, times the speed of light, becomes quite clear but also truly complicated for those who are not used to diving into the concepts of Physics. Therefore, for this book we shall focus mostly on the factors energy and mass and highlight the relevant message that we need to grasp to understand the importance of energy in our lives and health.

E stands for *energy*, **m** stands for *mass* and c^2 stands for the *speed of light* squared. Energy and mass are interchangeable; they are the manifestation of the same thing, mass presents itself in a more crystalized form of energy. Therefore, everything is energy!

This concept remained with me for days. I could *understand* it because I had studied Physics and Biology in school, so I knew about atoms, but I could not fully *absorb* it as somehow, I felt that this energy was outside of me, that what I had learned in school was about a universe far away from me. I knew I had atoms within my constitution, but I doubted whether these atoms were common to the whole universe. In school, Physics and Biology were taught as separate subjects: references were made between the two, but I was never told that I was energy. Does this sound familiar?

It was clear to me at this point that I had to understand this concept of universal energy quickly, because the energy that Einstein was referring to was in everything, creating fields and waves, connecting and posting a message to the universe that would reflect my goals, present feelings and thoughts. It was therefore crucial to emanate waves of the reality I wanted to achieve.

The reality that I wanted was to get better and to feel balanced. Therefore, it was of great importance to vibrate in this healthy frequency to obtain 'my' reality.

So, a deeper journey into science started ... "Why are we energy?"

Throughout the centuries many people have asked this question and advanced numerous explanations, some more scientific, others more spiritual or religious. I am not going to discuss right or wrong here, because the more we look into it the more we realise that the essence of these different approaches is the same: a pure infinite intelligence is behind our existence. These diverse approaches are simply different musical instruments playing the same melody: "(…) everyone who is seriously involved in the pursuit of science becomes convinced that some spirit is manifest in the laws of the universe, one that is vastly superior to that of man." Albert Einstein (To Phyllis Wright, January 24, 1936, in DEAR PROFESSOR EINSTEIN ed. by Alice Calaprice, pp. 128-129, Einstein Archives 42- 602).

However, I will guide you to look at Einstein's message that energy and mass are equivalent in greater detail.

What was Einstein telling us and how does it directly relate to us? Well, it explains what we are and how we can find our uniqueness and balance with the world around us by simply *being* energy. But how did he arrive at this conclusion?

Let's go back in time, and as we do so, I will highlight at the end of each analysis the thoughts and conclusions that I took as part of the frequency that I needed to find my place in the universe.

▬ NEWTON ▬▬▬▬▬▬▬▬▬▬▬▬▬▬▬

Between the years 1687 and 1915 our best understanding of the universe and gravity was that proposed by Sir Isaac Newton. As you know, the force of gravity has both strength and direction, and in our everyday lives we feel a force basically pointing towards the centre of the Earth. According to Newton, Earth's gravity stretches far away, literally throughout the universe, though it grows weaker the further away you get. As the Earth moves, its gravitational field instantly changes with it, everywhere in the universe.

However, Newton couldn't fully explain how this happened and he had no space-time relation in his process of understanding the universe. He couldn't fully explain how the universe 'communicated' within itself to keep its balance or whether this balance would take time or not.

This conflict in Newton's physics was present because his entire perspective was based on the theory that there exists only matter and nothing else: the whole universe was a machine, made of matter, and so were we. Therefore, according to Newtonian physics, life forms are like machines in that you can take them apart and put them back together and learn about their functions. Newton had a concept of atoms, but these were solid.

Even though this approach might work for certain things, when we consider a living being and its different connections to everything, this approach is, in my opinion, soulless!

Although this approach is still very present in our everyday lives and of great importance in certain areas of our everyday living, when we look at our health and life as a whole, this theory is no longer sufficient to explaining the miracle of living. Even though medical science is still somehow stuck in the Newtonian concept of matter and new physics is still being avoided in medical schools, the rest of science has now moved on to Quantum Physics. The world is no longer simply seen as a machine, and that is thanks to Einstein's Theory of Relativity.

▬ THEORY OF RELATIVITY ▬▬▬▬▬

Albert Einstein presented a theory that would change our perception of the universe forever. Indeed, even though a hundred years have passed, physicists are still studying his equations and referring to his researches.

On the 25th November of 1915, when Einstein submitted a paper with all of his field equations to the Royal Prussian Academy of the Natural Sciences, he knew that he had achieved his goal: the New Law of General Gravity that would supersede Isaac Newton's law of gravity.

What was new about this theory?

I will break down the general approach to his theory in **three parts**, but please understand that these three parts interrelate and constitute a whole.

FIRST PART

The starting point of this theory is the <u>special relativity</u> that mass and energy are equivalent, which means that mass is the same as energy.

What Einstein is saying is that from the very beginning of his search for this new law of gravity, he had as his starting point the special relativity that mass and energy are equivalent, everything is energy: you, me, the trees, the plants, the stones, the water and the entire universe.

How is that possible, you're thinking?

Everything around us has as its base of existence small particles of energy called atoms, not the solid Newtonian concept of atoms, but atoms that move in waves. These tiny particles are nowadays called 'vortexes' of energy, because although they have a nucleus consisting of protons and neutrons, these even smaller particles are nothing more than pure energy.

They also have electrons within their constitutions, and with that they move and connect to each other to form different molecules. If we focus on ourselves as an example, these molecules will turn into cells, the cells will turn into tissues, the tissues will turn into organs and the organs will make our bodies. So that's it, **we are light/energy, just**

vibrating in a lower energetic frequency that is perceived by our brain as physical!

Therefore, because of the atoms and the fields of energy they create, we and everything around us is energy. The base of existence is entirely the same within the universe. It flows and blends, because the universe exists in a harmonic balance that governs all things and dimensions.

My Conclusions

When I finished analysing this part of Einstein's theory of relativity, not with the eyes of a physicist but with the eyes of a woman just trying to find the frequency of her healthy reality, I realised that as a base of my existence I had a tiny spark of energy that carried within it life. This small spark created different molecules that, depending on the way they 'got together', would create different forms of life.

We have trillions of atoms vibrating inside ourselves and these atoms are the same as the ones that created everything around us. These atoms are intelligent and they still carry within their constitution the vibration of the universe.

Because in Physics *energy cannot* be created or destroyed, it can only be changed from one form to another, this base of life transforms itself into a physical body that in turn will vibrate in different types of emanations, from organ functions to thought processes and emotions, all connected to the universe. How? That was my next question. Continue reading and let's find the answer together.

(No wonder I feel at home when I look at the stars, when I give myself the chance to calm down, to connect. I am a part of it all!).

SECOND PART

Gravity is warped and curves in the fabric of space and time.

We have considered atoms and how they are the base of everything that exists in the universe. However, within these atoms exist even smaller particles. This 'quanta base' of the universe is what many call the matrix, the base of it all, the beginning of everything, a base that still exists and that travels around the universe carrying within itself the secret of life. A base, that is also a part of us, vibrating in every single one of the trillions of atoms that constitute our body.

There are several theories about this energy base, one of them being String Theory, but no matter what, the base of the macro-cosmos vibrates within our micro-cosmos, hence within us we have the universe, literally!

These particles of energy create a gravitational field that holds information about everything that has happened and everything that is happening. It actually holds and balances the universe in a way that transcends space and time.

This gravitational field holds the universe together and like the fabric of a trampoline, it curves and adapts to the changes and movements that are constantly occurring. We are all held by this gravity and within itself this gravity holds the information to keep the balance of life, connecting everything to everything, including us.

My Conclusions

A gravitational field that holds and connects everything and that has within its base the same energetic sparks that I possess made it clear to me that I am a vibrational being connected to a vibrational world, constantly receiving and emanating energy. When I finished analysing this part of Einstein's theory I felt whole, a part of it all.

I can't therefore feel complete merely through food and exercise. I can't feel complete just by thinking positively and cleansing my emotions ... I need to go 'home'. And this 'home' made me, it knows me; it balances everything, creating homeostasis in the whole of the universe.

I am a part of this, you are a part of this, and feeling this connection and being guided by this connection is normal, because the trees, the birds, the animals, the water, they all do it. It's in their (our) 'energetic DNA'!

This gravitational fabric warps and curves, balancing planets, stars, people ... it's all around us. But my next question was "how does this gravitational field 'read' what is happening to me"?

THIRD PART

This gravitational field of energy will create gravitational waves, or according to Einstein, ripples.

Given what we have analysed, it comes as no surprise that within this gravitational fabric there are different types of vibrations. This is the result of energy's unique capacity to change and transform. An example of those vibrations closer to us and to our living would be the one emanated from our body. Our body produces a magnetic field as a result of the workings of our entire system. A simple example of this is our thought process. All mental activity involves electromagnetic energy.

The neurotransmitters are created only when electrical impulses induce a voltage in a neuron that exceeds the firing threshold of the nerve. Now if we understand that we have billions of neurons throughout our body it won't be very hard to accept **that mental activity can be effectively analysed and monitored entirely by electromagnetic principles.** We can compare this to electrical engineering, where all currents moving through a wire produce electromagnetic fields around them.

There are nevertheless other frequencies and vibrations emanating within 'our' gravitational field, such as physical body activity (heartbeat, organs working…) and emotions. These all create lower or higher levels of frequencies and emanate sounds or colours. Everyone around you vibrates like this!

Consequently, ripples of energy with information are constantly being emanated and this information, or waves, get entangled and connected, travelling at the speed of light. This is not an assumption; this is a fact of science.

Let's imagine an example for a moment: you are supposed to meet someone in their office and as you arrive you feel something is wrong. No one is arguing, the place is organised, but your whole body is telling you that you shouldn't relax.

Later on you find out that a serious argument occurred in that office a few hours before you arrived. People were screaming, shouting and there was even some physical confrontation between some of the people involved. What you felt as you arrived were the ripples of energy emanated by what had happened.

The information stayed in the air and your magnetic field picked it up and informed your whole system to be aware. Everything you think, feel and do vibrates in your magnetic field. We are surrounded by ripples of energy carrying information about everything that is happening.

Our body and mind are in permanent conversation with the ripples around ourselves and with the gravitational fabric that supports everything in the universe. This magnetic field carries a print of what created the universe (the matrix energy, or God if you prefer), but also a print of everything that exists in the universe, and that includes us.

Let me give you another example, now at a larger scale and not so close to our gravitational field.

Until 2015, Einstein's theory of relativity had been proven correct in levels around us, for example ripples of gravity generated by our magnetic fields. However, for it to be absolutely proven we would have to identify waves coming from very far away in the universe. That is what happened in 2015.

A team of scientists announced on 14th September 2015 that they had heard and recorded the sound of two black holes colliding a billion light-years away, and this was described as "a fleeting chirp that fulfilled the last prediction of Einstein's general theory of relativity."(New York Times, Feb.11 2016) It proved that Einstein's gravitational field theory was no longer a theory; it was a **fact**.

Gravitational waves, Einstein's ripples in space time, were as mentioned, spotted for the first time on 14th September 2015, at 9:50:45 universal time.

This discovery was a great triumph for the 1,000 physicists with the Laser Interferometer Gravitational-Wave Observatory (LIGO), a pair of gigantic instruments in Hanford, Washington, and Livingston, Louisiana.

My Conclusions

As the base of my being is energy and this energy transforms itself within me in different ways, emanating different levels of frequencies (higher or lower), the whole of me is not only directly connected to the universe, but it can also pick up on the magnetic fields that surround me. It can read them and find guidelines to direct me on the best path to a true and unique me.

Taking into consideration that my whole body is prepared to process this information and transform it into mental thoughts and emotions, I can safely say that I have an internal GPS that can take me anywhere, because it knows me and it can help me vibrate within the frequency that I need and thus deal with the different challenges of life on this planet.

Being aware of our feelings and intuition is natural to human beings because we all have energy within us and we can pick up on energy. Living in tune with your body and soul is natural and crucial to a complete and fulfilling life.

By this stage of my journey through the theory of relativity I felt very confident that if I ate healthy food, vibrating with goodness and with my energy (I checked for food intolerances, allergies and ate according to my body's needs), I would be fine. If I cleared out blocked thought processes that weren't vibrating within the energy of what

I wanted to achieve, I would be fine. If I dealt with my emotions within the same energy of life and within my goal for balance in mind, and if I gave my body and mind the chance to connect to different levels of consciousness by listening and absorbing the energy of 'home', I would be fine.

We are such a complete and amazing miracle that every time I talk about it in my workshops or with my clients I feel emotional. Discovering this fact about myself, about us, was the best thing that could have happened in my life. I respect myself and the world around me so much more, and giving 100% to life isn't hard.

Nevertheless, be aware that each person has a different 100%. We are unique in our vibration and it is important to vibrate our own energy. So, give it your best in the ever-changing moments of your life, do it your own way, but never lose sight of the universal love that surrounds life.

'Physically' made to connect to different frequencies

After 'absorbing' Einstein's theory of relativity and accepting the flow of energy in every dimension of my life, I wanted to obtain a clearer understanding of the way my 'physical' body worked. This would allow me to balance energetically the four different levels of my existence and find the healthy frequency that I needed to emanate. In a talk with W. Hermanns, Einstein said: "I admit that thoughts influence the body" (in A Talk with Einstein, October1945, Einstein Archives 55-285) and he was correct. It was time to learn more!

I had made dietary changes, I was trying meditation, studying, re-correcting thought processes, I felt supported and loved, but I needed a base. A base that would give me a chance to organise all of the changes I was making in my life, but also a base from where I could energetically emanate a vibration that would then transform itself into a frequency of positivity and naturally blend with the life particles of the lovely natural food I was eating.

21

I found this base in the brain. Indeed, I had decided to research how my brain absorbed and represented my reality. I knew that after understanding this process, I would be able to rewrite my frequency with positivity. This would be the base that, through neurotransmissions, would 'post' my message in a way that all the cells in my body would hear.

We are beings of energy, constantly transforming and emanating different types of energy; and we are also made to read, understand and write energetic messages. More than what we believe and more than what we can sometimes conceive, we are a complete micro-cosmos in the larger macro-cosmos of life.

How does our micro-cosmos perceive the reality around us?

I will answer this question from two perspectives. The first will guide us to the way we form internal representations of ourselves and of the reality around us. Using the second we will dive into our 'emotional brain' and analyse in some detail how these internal representations get processed, and the influence they have in our health and well-being.

You will understand the impact that our representations of the world around us have in our lives and how we can change these representations to healthier, more positive ones, in the process changing our perceptions of ourselves and of our reality.

These perspectives that we are about to consider will be largely focused on the ways in which we vibrate 'physically', but never forget that we are energy and by absorbing a positive input you will emanate a more positive frequency, enabling your cells to vibrate in a healthier atmosphere that will be shared with the world around you through your magnetic field.

We will approach these perspectives in three steps.

FIRST STEP

How the brain absorbs information

Every second our brains receive more than 2,000,000 bits of information. This information is perceived by our brain through our senses and as a result our neurons will process and transmit the information throughout our body.

This means that per second, billions of bits of information *move around* our brain, and when this information is processed and absorbed we will create an internal representation of ourselves and our reality. This phase is part of what we call our *communication system*.

The communication system:

First the information gets filtered through the mind's filtering system (beliefs, memories, values, language, decisions).

Second some of this information will be deleted, distorted or generalised. Our brain can only **absorb** 134 bits of information per second, so if it is receiving more than 2,000,000 bits of information it needs to find ways of handling it.

Third we create an internal representation. This is achieved through feeling, taste, smell and sound. All these senses will determine our focus and representation of the information we received.

Fourth this internal representation will lead to a state. If the information looks good, for example it smells great or tastes nice, our state will be a happy one!

Fifth if psychologically we feel happy, this will lead to

a behaviour that will represent just that: a smile, hug or kiss, for example. If psychologically we feel unhappy, our behaviour will reflect that emotion instead.

Every single day of our lives is absorbed and memorised like this. Every day we feel our life this way, emanating positive or less positive frequencies through our thoughts and feelings.

Every day our bodies absorb information that will either make us feel balanced and a part of the whole, or in contrast feel blocked and stagnant. Our daily actions and reactions are a result of this communication system, which means that every day we are given a chance to re-correct our approach to life and act more positively.

Therefore, we are not stuck, we can change our internal representations and by doing this we will change the way in which we see ourselves and the reality around us. We will change the way our cells vibrate and understand our feelings, and life will blossom in a harmonic dance with the gravitational field that involves us.

We are body, mind and spiritual beings. Our mind and body work together to make this journey in life happy, loving, successful and curious, always connecting us to the whole. The more we know about how our body and mind work, the greater our ability to achieve the goals our true self wants us to achieve.

In the past, when people spoke about the mind they referred to the brain. However, today we know that the mind is everywhere within us. We know that we have billions of neurons in our body and that through synaptic connections the cells talk with each other.

Therefore, instead of thinking negative thoughts – "I'm

not good enough to do this!" – I can think positively and offer my brain the chance to rewrite my reality: "I have within myself all the tools I need to learn new things. I am a capable person and an important piece in the whole of the universe".

Our thoughts and emotions travel from the brain and are absorbed as a stimulus all over our body, and so it is crucial that we monitor our thoughts as much as we monitor what we eat. The more positive inputs I give myself, the healthier I will be. Subsequently, this positivity will be emanated to the universe, presenting the possibility of attracting similar emanations, entangling itself with similar magnetic fields. This is the law of attraction.

I see this as a never-ending journey to finding who we are, how we see others, and how we can always learn more, do better and be the happy person we want to be.

As Louise Hay argued, "What makes our reality are just thoughts and thoughts can be changed."(Louise Hay was a metaphysical lecturer and teacher who sold more than 50 million books worldwide. She was the founder of Hayhouse).

SECOND STEP

How the brain processes the communication system

Our brain can be divided into three principal parts:

- <u>Neo-cortex</u>: thinking, logic and planning. It is our conscious mind.
- <u>Limbic system</u>: emotions, values and judgments. This part of the brain is also called the emotional brain.

- <u>Reptilian complex</u>: the breathing, heartbeat. This is the "fight or flight" response and we've inherited it from reptiles.

The communication system we have discussed is processed in these different parts of the brain, but the one part of the brain that is key in this daily representation of ourselves and of our world is the Limbic System.

The limbic system has within its constitution several parts that play an important role in processing new information and relating it with past memories. It deals with senses and emotions and has a major influence in the workings of our endocrine system and autonomic nervous system.

The hippocampus, thalamus, hypothalamus and amygdala are the basic structure of the limbic system. However, in this book I will also refer to the pineal gland and the pituitary gland in particular, even though they are found within the structure of the hypothalamus.

The structure of the limbic system nevertheless raises debate, and a consensus on how it should be presented has yet to be reached. However, keeping in tune with the goal of this book, analysis will be simple and straightforward.

The hippocampus is a small organ located in the brain's temporal lobe and represents an important part of our limbic system. It plays a crucial role in memory and the attainment of knowledge. It helps us to consolidate information from short-term memory to long-term memory, but it also deals with spatial memory, helping us find our way around.

What the hippocampus does is shape our conscious thinking and mediates learnt responses from the past with new information. By considering all of these functions, one can easily understand the importance of this structure for establishing new and positive internal representations.

The hippocampus is critical to processing our everyday information. Damage can lead to mild cognitive issues, as well as more serious ones related to dementia and Alzheimer's disease.

The thalamus relays the information absorbed by our senses (touch, hearing and taste) and sends it to the different parts of the brain where it can be processed, including the cerebral cortex.

The sense of smell is not processed by the thalamus; amazingly this sense has its own structure within the limbic system, called the olfactory cortex.

That childhood memory of the appetising smell of a cake being baked by your mother? That one memory that takes you back every time someone is baking? That happens because your sense of smell directly activates your limbic system and quickly relates the new input to past memories.

This is also the reason why using essential oils can be a powerful aid in physical and emotional healing, as well as helping you to meditate.

The hypothalamus is responsible for the production of many of the body's essential hormones (these are chemical substances that help control different cells and organs). The hormones from the hypothalamus govern physiological functions such as temperature regulation, thirst, hunger, sleep, mood and sex drive, and the release of other hormones in the body.

Within this area of the brain we can also find the pituitary gland and pineal gland, and all three help balance the endocrine system. The hypothalamus' main function is homeostasis, and so it aims to keep our body within its internal balance.

The pituitary gland, also known as the hypophysis, is a pea-sized lump of tissue connected to the inferior portion of the hypothalamus of the brain. Many vessels surround the pituitary gland to carry the hormones it releases throughout the body.

Its main function is to regulate body chemistry. This gland regulates emotion and intellect, working hand in hand with the pineal gland and the hypothalamus to achieve overall balance.

The pineal gland is also very small, the size of a grain of rice, and was for many years a mystery to the medical world. More mystical or holistic approaches to health viewed this gland as the "seat of the soul". This idea emerged in the 17th century with the French philosopher, René Descartes.

In Energy therapies this gland is of great importance as it is related to the third eye chakra located at the centre of the forehead between the eyebrows. The third eye chakra primarily affects the pineal gland as well as the cerebellum, and its energies are associated with clairvoyance, sensitivity, intuition and intellectual activity.

The pineal gland produces the hormone melatonin, which helps regulate the human sleep-wake cycle known as the circadian rhythm. It is known as our internal "body clock".

The activity of the pineal gland is inhibited by stimulation from the photoreceptors of the retina. This light sensitivity causes melatonin to be produced only in low light or darkness. Increased melatonin production causes humans to feel drowsy at night-time when the pineal gland is active.

Nevertheless, it has recently been discovered that the pineal gland secretes another hormone, serotonin. Serotonin, which is as important to waking activities as melatonin is to sleepiness, serves several functions, including the regulation of attention. Serotonin is among the substances responsible for the ability of a human with a healthily functioning brain to filter out background noise and sensory data. It is also known to moderate our perception of pain: less serotonin means lower tolerance to pain in our bodies.

Essentially, the pineal gland governs (and when necessary inhibits) the functions of the pituitary gland, and it is the balancing of these two glands that helps facilitate the opening to different levels of consciousness.

They are interlinked in their work controlling the endocrine system, and for fun I call them the generals that control our army of hormones!

Together, these different structures that constitute our 'emotional brain' keep us in harmony, physically and emotionally but also mentally. By sharing the necessary information with the cerebral cortex, they will also affect our conscious thinking and decision-making.

Remember, these processes happen as a whole, and bring the different levels of our existence into such a profound bond that if one is unbalanced, the others should always be taken into consideration in the process of rebalancing.

I believe that by understanding what this part of your brain does, you will possess an amazing base to start structuring the changes you want to implement in your life. Just by giving yourself a positive input with a constructive thought or a loving emotion, you will be providing the first step for your body to feel good and open to change. This is because that input will be sent from your brain to the rest of your body, telling each cell that you are positively changing things in your life.

However, the limbic system does much more than this, holding in its structure another key to healthy leaving that I find important to address before finishing this chapter.

What I am about to describe to you will take you to the next level of understanding: how the four levels that we have been discussing work together to keep you healthy.

As discussed at the beginning of this second step, another part of the structure of the limbic system is the amygdala. The amygdala is the part of the brain that will activate your "fight or flight" mode, also called the sympathetic nervous system.

The autonomic nervous system that controls the automatic aspects of our body such as circulation, breathing, heart rate, digestion and blood pressure is divided into two parts: the parasympathetic nervous system and the sympathetic nervous system.

The "fight or flight" system is designed to protect our survival. It is activated any time there is a threat to our existence. It is our most basic survival mechanism and it runs on an unconscious level.

Our brain will perceive something as dangerous in many ways, ranging from a physical attack or accident to toxins in the body as well as emotions. For instance, in our brain we have toxin receptors that are triggered when toxins like pesticides, bacteria, yeast and heavy metals are able to cross the blood-brain barrier. When this happens, the amygdala is stimulated and emotions like fear, anxiety, anger and even pain can be activated. You are now functioning in "fight or flight" mode!

The sympathetic nervous system works hand in hand with the parasympathetic nervous system and if everything is working normally, when the threat to our survival passes the parasympathetic system is supposed to take over and turn off the sympathetic system, enabling our body to return to working 'normally'.

Unfortunately, this change doesn't always happen. Due to pollution, toxins, pesticides and stress the amygdala can become overactive, the consequences of which are potentially serious. This is why living a balanced lifestyle with 'clean' (non-processed) eating and exercise is so important.

However, because the amygdala, alongside the hippocampus, is also responsible for the **perception of toxic emotions** (anger, fear, stress and sadness) and relates them to past similar experiences, it is also important to absorb our reality with as much positivity and community support as possible. Remember, just by offering your hippocampus a loving, healthy thought, you will be informing every single cell of your body that change is possible and that you can change for the better.

When this doesn't happen and over-activity occurs, digestion and circulation can become impaired, blood pressure and heart rate rise, and cognitive abilities and memory may also be disturbed. Sleep and the detoxification system will be affected, and subsequently a decline in immune function will occur and neurotransmitters will be exhausted. When this situation goes unattended, absolute fatigue sets in because cortisol levels become depleted and can no longer meet the demands of the permanent stress. That's how important balance, love and positive living are for our health!

Even though the limbic system and its functions had seemed so complete and critical to my healthy path and everyday positive thinking, learning about the amygdala transferred the importance of positive thinking for positive feeling to the next level. It transformed the importance of balancing the 'whole' of me into a priority, forcing me to find clear solutions to keep my parasympathetic system in control of my body as much as possible.

I was absolutely blown away by the fact that through my emotions and mental thinking, my internal representations of the world around me and of myself had such an influence on my health. To hear about it, to understand it energetically was already a strong impetus for my journey towards health, but to realise that effectively my whole hormonal system and nervous system paid as much attention to what I was feeling and thinking as to what I was eating and how I was living made me want to do even more. I had established dietary changes; the awareness of how I thought and felt was on full mode. I was exercising, loving and spending time with the people who supported me. The only other thing required for the push was meditation. Once again, I found the extra input I needed in the limbic system.

With the help of the pineal gland, working within the structure of the hypothalamus, the limbic system gives us the chance to let go of our conscious worries and stress. It helps us to meditate!

So, when you breathe in deeply, your body will produce positive hormones. You close your eyes and in a relaxing environment with dim light, you calm yourself down to connect with your unconscious mind. Comfortable and relaxed, this amazing brain structure will take you away to meditation, filtering out background noise and helping you to relieve stress.

The more you activate your pineal gland, the faster this meditative process will occur, giving you the chance to listen to yourself and allowing your atoms to connect with the universal energy. This is our own internal GPS to meditation and to 'home', and a great example of how we are 'physically' made to connect to higher frequencies of energy.

This system helps us to cleanse stagnant thoughts and emotions through balancing melatonin and serotonin, and in our unconscious mind allows us to bring positive thoughts and positive outcomes to our problems, whilst gently calming negative inputs. Moreover, when meditation is insufficient, and hypnosis represents the solution, this part of the brain will yet again guide us in our process of positive change.

I was meditating, but after grasping the overall influence of this practice, meditation became a daily routine that I knew I couldn't do without.

Our physical existence starts with incredibly small particles that, like seeds, carry within themselves everything that we need to become the human miracles that we are. Somehow these particles accumulate in a dance of physical metamorphosis and emotions, constantly communicating with the universe. We are energy, we transform energy, we produce energy, we communicate in energy and we feel all these energies. Our body functions, heals, thinks, feels, by existing in this energetic abundance. Our 'emotional brain' is an example of that.

The importance of the limbic system in the representation of our everyday world is astonishing. Yes, it's true that the brain works as a whole and that this is just one part of it. However, I was looking for a base and this is a very powerful base. Now you know about it too!

THIRD STEP

More about meditation

Using meditation as a complementary tool to support your positive change in eating a healthy diet, expressing curiosity, creativity and doing physical exercise, is the perfect way to bring together all of the pieces that will help you complete the puzzle of your health and vibrate in a positive frequency.

Research has demonstrated through brain scans that through this holistic approach your amygdala will shrink over time and the "fight or flight" triggers will be reduced. What's more, the hippocampus will actually increase over time.

Healthy living and meditation have been shown to have a calming effect on the body/mind system and help promote a relaxed parasympathetic state of the autonomic nervous system. As we've seen, this state is crucial for the immune system to be able to heal and maintain this healing.

Nine years ago, when I sat down to meditate in the terrace, I didn't know that my sympathetic system was overactive. My body was dealing with toxins, bacteria, yeast and heavy metals, and because it wasn't calming down and detoxing, stress mode was always active.

I was also feeling sad, stressed and scared, so when I sat down and started to relax, my body absorbed the light and my limbic system took me away into meditation. It calmed down my systems and helped my mind spread good thoughts and feelings throughout my body, activating the parasympathetic system and calming down the pain.

That's why mediation offers so many benefits to our health and that's why accepting that we are energy and that we can read and listen to the different magnetic fields that surround us is no joke or fantasy. It's a reality and an extremely important aid to healthy, happy leaving.

On that day I listened to my body and didn't go to bed, and that was the best decision I could have ever made. It brought me here and I am healthy and smiling at life!

When we're stressed, ill or unhappy we need to approach our recovery by supporting the four levels that constitute our existence: physical, mental, emotional and spiritual. We need to take control and bring the parasympathetic system into its normal state, giving ourselves the chance to regenerate, and this can only be done when all the levels are addressed within the same 'healthy and positive' frequency. That way we can match the frequency of the reality we want and achieve our goal. We are physically built for that.

Just a note:

Meditation can be a very profound practice and one can stay in this meditative state for a long time. Some people will meditate daily for half an hour, others one hour or more. However, some can only do it for five or ten minutes and that is just fine.

There can be very specific rituals, mantras and sutras to help you meditate, but I find that instead of helping, these tools sometimes become an excuse _not_ to do it. Therefore, don't worry about time or how ... just let yourself go with your favourite music. Find your inner voice and then make it a regular practice to be with yourself.

One of the things that I do for my clients and for myself is to record a small meditation with the 'message' they need to hear. It's never longer than fifteen minutes and it can be as short as five minutes. When done regularly, short, straightforward meditation can be the key to finding yourself and can open the door to your spiritual self. It is such an amazing experience. Give it a go!

Einstein's science and energy therapies

If we bring all the information about energy that we've been exploring and relate it to our daily routine and to the many natural therapies that we now have at our disposal, we can explain away the doubts that still arise about how modalities like Reiki, Chakra balancing, energy balancing, Hypnosis and Acupuncture work.

When we go for a Reiki treatment, for example, and here I stipulate that it must be a trained and balanced practitioner, this practitioner is actually picking up on the magnetic field and the ripples of information that are emanated by our body (physical, emotional and mental activities), and connects them to the matrix energy (more spiritual). Because this energy carries knowledge, it *can help balance* any blockages in our energetic body. It is with the help of the limbic system that this process is fully activated, and because the frequency of our body changes, the message sent throughout the cells will support a more 'physical' balance. The same with Reconnective Healing (RH), Energy Balancing and Acupuncture, because the Chinese meridians are pathways of energy.

However, when I say that it *can help balance*, I mean that the energy is ours. This practitioner can give the push to a more 'matrix oriented' energy, and if we understand that we can balance our energy by eating healthily, exercising, cleaning our emotions, letting go of restrictive thought processes and opening up to different levels of consciousness, then we will be on our way to healing and healthy living.

Seeing someone that can help us balance the several levels of our existence is important, but the key is to learn to balance it ourselves. We must accept that the body is ours, the energy is ours and that there is no one better than us to find our healthy path.

Yes, Einstein's gravitational field theory has been scientifically proven, and with that chakras and auras become clear emanations of energy. However, science has also established that it is very important that each person understand that he or she is energy and that through energy you can balance your whole self. Indeed, as we've been learning, energy is the common denominator at every single level of our existence.

We have seen that energy manifests itself physically, mentally, emotionally and spiritually, so all of these energetic levels **need** to be balanced in the **same vibration**, but in different ways.

If we eat real food, it vibrates with our body because it isn't processed, and we will feel healthier. Likewise, if we exercise and take care of our body. By achieving this we will feel better mentally and if we are open to learning new things and activating our brain positively, we will feel a strong energetic harmony, physically, mentally and even emotionally.

By clearing blocked emotions, resentments, fears, doubts and old emotional patterns that restrict us, we will harmonise these levels even further. However, this is not enough: the matrix energy vibrates within us and so making time to connect with it is essential for harmonious existence.

Science is now discovering the importance of this and has reinforced the notion with considerable research. Meditation is now fully accepted as an essential practice. Yoga, tai chi, chi kung and mindfulness are also examples of this approach to more connected living.

Offering our mind and body regular opportunities to vibrate in a higher frequency can not only bring to light blockages in our unconscious mind that we wouldn't even know about, but also guide us to a positive future. It connects us to our higher self, a part of ourselves that we seldom listen to and that is as much a part of us as our body. Neuro-linguistic processing (NLP), along with more Western approaches, is also a great tool to achieving this connection with our optimal self.

It is true that numerous approaches to health and achieving balance exist, but all we have to do is pick the one that can bring us the 'whole' we need and incorporate it into our lives. Whatever you do, don't close your mind to the Energy Therapies that are now at your disposal. Find one that vibrates with you; just make sure to have a balanced, healthy practitioner guiding you in your journey.

Ironically, and this is my opinion, science is actually bringing our general sense of God to the equation of the universe and is guiding us to the divinity within ourselves, because if we do not lose ourselves in the endless discussions that science and physics raise, its base connects us with one another, our planet and with the universe.

My children have been taught in Biology that we are 97% stardust and this is a fact. So next time you look up at the sky to see the stars, understand that they shine within you and that, maybe, just maybe, the stars from up there are looking at you and saying:

"Those stars down there are so beautiful. Look how they shine. They are walking miracles!"

Balance is the key

We are vibrational beings vibrating in a vibrational world. Within us are lower energetic frequencies (more connected to the physical) and higher energetic frequencies (more connected to the spiritual), and the more we are aware that we are 'made' to vibrate with both equally, hand in hand, simultaneously, the easier it will be to 'balance' joyfully through life.

Is one frequency better than the other? No, they are both magical in the existence that they can offer us. However, the higher you go the more connected you will be to the matrix energy or to God and the divine, bringing a sense of oneness and loving that a more physical existence may not be able to achieve. Therefore, by balancing both, we can bring that sense to our life on earth and vibrate in a more wholesome way.

However, let's imagine for a moment that we could separate the two frequencies. Is being physical, because it vibrates in a lower energetic frequency, less magical?

Many people ask me this and many try so hard to achieve higher frequencies that they neglect their bodies. Let me take you on a short lower frequency tour and analyse this point by looking at its miraculous emanations.

The 'physical' frequency takes space; it has more condensed particles of energy that can be perceived by our brain as physical, material. This lower frequency can be touched ... touched, isn't that wonderful?

Close your eyes and imagine touching someone you love. Touch, feel it on your skin, embrace it! Amazing, isn't it?

Look at yourself, touch your hands, your mouth, your nose, hear your heart beat, feel the warmth of your skin. What an overwhelming miracle. What a miraculous way of being, vibrating in a lower frequency!

And then there are the colours ... flowers, fruit, paintings. Absorb the colours with your eyes. 'Absorb' the colours with your nose. 'Absorb' the colours with your mouth. Is it not magical?!

It's true that every sense will connect you with a chain of thoughts and emotions that will guide you to a higher frequency, but don't think about that now, stay vibrating low.

When you drink a cup of tea with herbs and spices, when you taste it, smell it, and the energetic particles of each ingredient touch your particles. This is also a uniqueness of this frequency, and it feels great!

It's fine to be here vibrating low and to be able to touch, to look, to feel life on Earth, to cherish it. This already represents a high-quality existence if you appreciate it, if you love it, if you feel it and take good care of it. To be able to express love with a smile, a hug, a kiss, a flower, a cake ... this is so profoundly, 'cellularly' magical and the universe needs that.

Now by being physical we can also think about things, ask questions, plant seeds, make a meal, and come up with equations to explain the world around us.

We build houses, cars (and let's not look at the negative side of these things, that's not the purpose of this book), computers, robotic legs, arms, hearts. These are 'lowerly' emanated frequencies and yet they are remarkable.

Then there's giving birth ... I'm a mother, and to physically create a human being, to bring it into the world, to vibrate with its existence and hold it, protect it with your arms, no words can express the emotion of it!

Nevertheless, existing in a lower frequency can also bring us moments when things seem stagnant and we feel stuck, unaware that much is happening in a higher frequency around us. That much is shifting, changing: every single emanation of energy is being rearranged so that a plan, a dream becomes a moment, a pure, intense moment of achievement and realisation.

We sometimes get lost in a lifeless existence; our bodies ache with our souls wanting to tell us about the rearrangements of the higher frequencies and how we can listen to them. This is why we cannot be *whole* without the connection to the *whole* of the energy, without all the frequencies emanating together.

Therefore, even though we isolated the physical frequency of our existence for just a moment and we saw its positivity, existing **only** in a lower frequency is not possible because every single part of us is connected to the macro-cosmos and therein exists balance, knowledge and, I believe, love. This love always wants to be connected, compassionate with every single frequency, so that the energy emanated vibrates in the whole of the universe. Without these, without us, the balance would not exist and the flow of life would be broken.

It all starts, as we've seen, at a subatomic level of vibration that is untouchable, invisible, but that nevertheless exists. A frequency so high that it carries knowledge and exists in a vibration of no space and time; a vibration so inconceivably small that one would never imagine it as the base of all things around us. This base vibrates in every single part of us and of the world around us.

This makes the existence of thoughts, emotions and spirituality within a physical body so outstanding, that the simple fact of just being here should be enough to appreciate who we are and where we have come from, and want to be the optimal vibration of our existence!

Conclusion

Many energies and different vibrations exist naturally within us. Our body and soul know what to do. Give them a chance…

Believing in God or not is not a key factor for you to believe in your energy. Believing in yourself and knowing where you come from is the key to help you in your journey in life. Find a path between the many approaches to a more meaningful life. Find a balance between Eastern and Western therapies; they are all pieces within the symphony of our existence and they can bring you the different melodies that your dance of life requires throughout your journey on this planet.

Above all, love yourselves, understand that within you there's a universal light that knows who you are because it made you, it manifests itself in everything, maintaining a balance with as much love and cooperation as possible.

Life is a constant conversation between us and the universe. Sometimes tears come our way, sometimes laughter, but the important thing is to learn, clean, listen and fly with the wind of gravity and without too much luggage!

Tips

Balancing the energy in our bodies and bringing more positive thought patterns into our lives can be achieved in numerous ways. Today there exist numerous books about how to support you in this change. I will, however, share with you a few tips to get you started, but don't forget, opening the doors to positive frequencies should be a daily routine, because the more you activate your unique energy, the more balanced you will be.

It does not have to be complicated; simple ways of bringing those frequencies to your life consciously and easily exist. Here are some of my ways of doing it. They are easy approaches, but their results are very powerful.

A CUP OF ENERGY FIRST THING IN THE MORNING

I believe that channelling white light and love to ourselves and to our homes every day is a great way of keeping our energy balanced. In my workshops a lot of people say that they find it difficult to meditate and that it's hard to take time to meditate. Therefore, I now always share this simple, mindful and loving exercise with my groups.

We all drink something in the morning, be it water, coffee or tea. Here I will use tea as an example because it's what I drink in the morning.

Choose some herbs that you like the smell of, such as lavender, rosemary, thyme, or lemon balm, or perhaps some ginger, lemon, cinnamon or star anise. Smell them and listen to what your body is asking for.

Warm some water and pick a cup that you like (you can even choose a specific colour that you feel attracted to at the time). Place the chosen herbs in the cup and add the warm water.

Wait a few minutes before you drink it, but while waiting smell the perfume emanating from the cup. Feel the warmth from the cup.

Close your eyes, breathe deeply, and think of someone you love or of something that brings you joy.

Stay for a moment, holding that feeling, let it slowly spread through your body and imagine that love and joy spreading around the room and then to your house and family!

When this feeling becomes strong and present, imagine a pure, beautiful, healing, loving white light coming from up very high in the heavens, coming through your head, and touching every single cell of your body. Let it travel through your body and once again spread to your home and family.

If you are ill, bring that light to the specific issue that you are dealing with and let it cleanse the energy. You can even do this for your workplace, school, and the emotional issues with which you are dealing. Just imagine the light, the love that you brought to your cup, the warmth and the perfume emanating from your herbs, and let it flow.

Breathe deeply again and say "I love myself and that's ok. I am one with the universe around me. Well is well and balanced".

Open your eyes and continue with your routine. This simple exercise can take just a few minutes or it can last longer if you wish to stay in the light longer. It is simple, and it involves your touch, your sense of smell and your emotions, making it easier for you to tune in with your inner self and your spirituality. Try it, little miracles have happened in my world with this quick cup of energy!

LISTEN TO MUSIC. TO 'YOUR' MUSIC

Listen to music: "Music gives a soul to the universe, wings to the mind, flight to the imagination and life to everything" (Plato). Listen to the music that makes you feel alive, which makes you want to dance, sing. Just by doing this you will be connecting to your own energy, expressing yourself and yes, meditating.

However, if what you want is to turn meditation into a deeper journey, pick a soft, gentle melody, but once again pick one that vibrates with you. It makes such a difference.

In my studio there is always music. It helps me to do my work better, but people seem to feel that they are transported to a different dimension when they come through the door, and they relax.

So, go and find your tune. Dance, meditate, and let the pineal gland and the pituitary gland guide you to the infinite intelligence. Do you know what will happen? Mentally and emotionally you will feel happier. Physically you will feel alive and energetically you will be more balanced and connected.

TALK WITH YOUR CEREBRAL CORTEX

One of the things that I give to each of my clients is a booklet and a pen. I encourage them to keep the booklet with them and to write down any negative thoughts and emotions that they feel are limiting the change they want to achieve. Under each negative note I recommend that they write a positive version of what they just expressed. If needed, this positive version can be repeated several times.

Limiting thought processes may have once been a positive strategy that helped us move forward, therefore it will take time to change these structures. It's important to be persistent in re-correcting our ways of thinking and feeling life.

Some people receive this tip with open arms; others struggle; still others draw instead of writing. Give it a go, see if it works for you.

TALK WITH YOUR AMYGDALA

I know this may sound crazy, but crazy is sometimes good, right? When I'm stressed and I feel that my heart beat is rising, I stop, breathe in deeply three times and talk with my amygdala. I say that I'm not in danger, that all is well, that I feel love for myself and that that love is spreading to the world around me. And then I continue to say that there's no need to activate the sympathetic system. I am safe and all is well ... and it works. I calm down!

BE GRATEFUL

I always encourage people to be grateful. Sometimes life throws so many challenges in our way that we forget to see the good around us and the good in us. I know this sounds very 'fashionable' at the moment, but the truth is that it is important to be aware of the positive things in our lives.

Pick a photo of someone or something that makes you feel good and a part of your path. Write positive things around it that make you smile and feel special. Put it in your wallet, on your fridge, hang it on the wall ... it doesn't matter, just give yourself the chance to feel grateful!

Express love for yourself. Hug a tree. Go for a walk. Be with the people you love. Live and be special.

Our journey together within the energy of this book has come to an end. I truly hope you feel special and more aware of your energetic vibration, and that with this awareness and tips you are able to find the special place that you are seeking. Doctors and therapists can help you in your path, but accept that you are also responsible for your health and for the way you absorb and vibrate in the reality around you. Your journey in life continues ... shine with all your atoms, be true to yourself, remember that *you are* a walking miracle!

EXTRA INFORMATION

Auras: For millions of years it has been believed that all objects, especially human and animal bodies, have an aura (or electromagnetic field), and that the aura can be visible to a trained eye. Many scientists, especially in the area of bioenergy informatics and using resonant field imaging have adopted this belief in their research and have tried to explain this phenomenon.

In the 19th century, metaphysical science introduced the theory that all things have a body of etheric substance, usually called the ethereal body. This body is composed of higher frequencies, which themselves are composed of subtle energy and of finer pre-matter quantum particles. These are very closely connected with the physical body because they are what generate matter. What subsequently happens is that these frequencies produce an electro field that comes through the quantum particles into the physical level.

"Body clock" or a biological clock is any sort of mechanism internal to an organism that governs its biological rhythms. The pineal gland is an example of those mechanisms. Internal clocks operate independently of the environment but are also affected by changes in environmental conditions.

"Chakra" is a Sanskrit word meaning "wheel". It is a wheel because it has a hub where many conduits of subtle energy intersect, and it has spokes, which are the radiations of subtle energy. It is thus a centre where subtle energy is concentrated. This subtle energy is the prana, the qui, the energy frequencies that we have been talking about along our journey and that can be specifically related to the concept of aura.

Although the human energy system is said to have many chakras, and new ones are being "discovered" all the time, the Hindu system refers to the seven major chakras. These seven chakras are located along the spine and the radiations of subtle energy spread through the nerves along our back, connecting this energy throughout the body. However, these chakras are by no means physical: they are energy. If you could see chakras, you would see each primary chakra as a spinning vortex or wheel of energy, spinning inward from the front of your body to the centre point of that chakra on the *kundalini* and then spinning outward to that same point from your back.

Homeostasis means keeping things constant and comes from two Greek words: 'homeo' meaning 'similar', and 'stasis' meaning 'stable'. A more formal definition of homeostasis is "the ability or tendency of a living organism, cell, or group to keep the conditions inside it the same despite any changes in the conditions around it, or this state of internal balance"- Cambridge Dictionary

Kundalini is the serpent goddess, according to Hindu tradition it is said to be coiled three-and-a-half times around the root chakra. When awakened, Kundalini pierces each chakra in turn as she travels from the root towards the crown. Once she has arrived at her destination the subject is said to have achieved enlightenment.

Neuro-linguistic processing (NLP): Dr Richard Bandler invented the term "Neuro-linguistic programming" in the 1970s, defining it as "a model of interpersonal communication chiefly concerned with the relationship between successful patterns of behaviour and the subjective experiences (esp. patterns of thought) underlying them" and "a system of alternative therapy based on this which seeks to educate people in self-awareness and effective communication, and to change their patterns of mental and emotional behaviour".

Neurons are nerve cells that process and transmit electrochemical signals; they are like lightning bolt transmitters/receivers/processers. The human brain has about 100 billion neurons and the rest of your body has many, many more.

Reiki reiki energy is described as having an intelligence of its own, flowing where it is needed in the client and creating the healing conditions necessary for the individual's needs. It cannot be guided by the mind; therefore, it is not limited by the experience or ability of the practitioner. However, I believe that this practitioner must vibrate in a balanced frequency to allow this healing energy to flow.

Reconnective healing (RH) is a new form of healing introduced by Dr. Eric Pearl and is seen as the new "Energy, Light and Information of our planet." (www. thereconnection.com-Official site)

We are stars: Using a technique called spectroscopy, a group of astronomers in Sloan Digital Sky Survey in New Mexico, have analysed more than 150.000 stars and concluded that both humans and the stars have in common 97% of the same kind of atoms.

Resources

http://energeticsinstitute.com.au/spiritual-concept-of-third-eye/

https://www.thoughtco.com/anatomy-of-the-brain-373479 https://eaware.org/pineal-gland/

http://www.sciencemag.org/news/2016/02/gravitational-waves-einstein-s-ripples-spacetimespotted-first-time

http://www.solarschools.net/resources/stuff/what_are_atoms.aspx https://plato.stanford.edu/entries/equivME/

http://www.einstein.caltech.edu/news/november-2015-dld.html

https://www.nytimes.com/2016/02/12/science/ligo-gravitational-waves-black-holeseinstein.html?_r=0

http://www.explainthatstuff.com/atoms.html

https://news.harvard.edu/gazette/tag/mindfulness-meditation/

https://www.health.harvard.edu/blog/relaxation-benefits-meditation-stronger-relaxation-benefitstaking-vacation-2

www.hsph.harvard.edu/nutritionsource/healthy-eating-plate/

www.ncbi.nlm.nih.gov/pubmed

www.associacaoportuguesadereiki.com/o-que-e-reiki/

www.reconexaoportugal.pt/

https://pnl-portugal.com

www.todabiologia.com/anatomia/homeostase.htm

https://www.google.com/amp/zeenews.india.com/space/stellar-discovery-human-bodies-are-97-percent-stardust-claim-scientists_1965852.html/amp#ampshare=http://zeenews.india.com/space/stellar-discovery-human-bodies-are-97-percent-stardust-claim-scientists_1965852.html

Inspiration:

www.hayhouse.com

kriscarr.com/

www.deepakchopra.com

www.jamieoliver.com

http://thichnhathanhfoundation.org

Important Note

Meditation can be the key to peacefulness and a more balanced thinking, but please be aware that it can also be a practise that can help you unblock emotions, fears and traumas. If you feel that this practise is making you feel uncomfortable and not able to deal with your emotions, please look for professional support with a qualified health care professional. We are made to let go of blocked emotions and stagnated thought processes, but sometimes professional support is needed for us to be able to overcome these patterns.

About the Author

Vanda is a Portuguese holistic therapist who dedicates her life in assisting people in their path by teaching them about Energy and Energy Therapies. Her simple approach to specific areas of Physics, Biology and Meditation, give each person the chance to discover their true vibration on this planet.

Printed in the United States
By Bookmasters